BOSTON

Text by

Bill Harris

Designed and Produced by

Ted Smart & David Gibbon

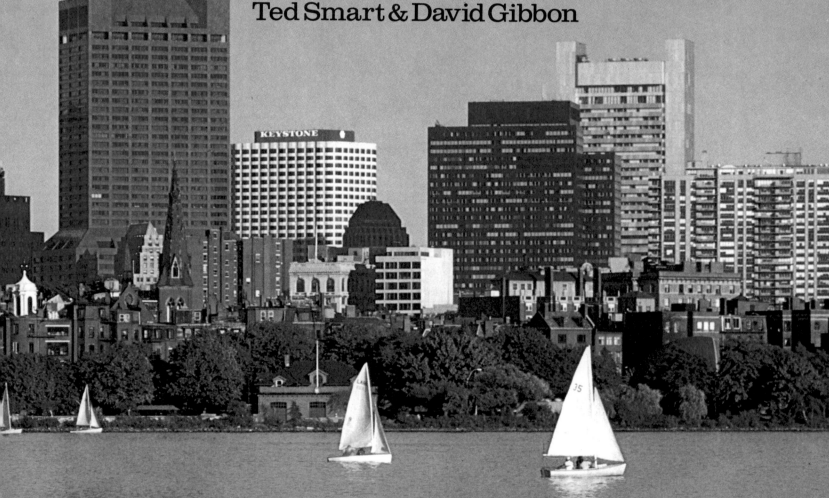

MAYFLOWER BOOKS · NEW YORK CITY

A FEW years ago, inspired by the success of the British TV series "Upstairs Downstairs," CBS Television produced a series of its own called "Beacon Hill."

The setting was Boston in the nineteen-twenties, and no expense was spared to make it historically accurate. Costumes were checked and rechecked with museum collections. Accents were refined to be just right. Antiques were brought in at great expense. The series was even filmed right on Beacon Hill, using exteriors at 89 Mount Vernon Street, one of the only houses on the Hill that isn't shoehorned in among its neighbors; the only one with a broad driveway.

But that wasn't the only thing that was different about TV's Beacon Hill. The story was about an upwardly-mobile Irish family – in the nineteen-twenties; any time before, or any time since, right up until the last twenty years or so, Irish families simply didn't live there.

Beacon Hill was the center of Boston society almost from the beginning when a silversmith named Paul Revere, a lawyer named James Otis, an importer named John Hancock and the richest man in the whole colony, Thomas Boylston, built small mansions there to take advantage of the view.

Today it's a neighborhood of steep, narrow streets lined with townhouses, many of which have long since been sub-divided into very high-priced apartments. Some ground floor shops are rented by sandal-makers and poster dealers, galleries and handicraft stores. Interspersed among them, occasional mansions designed by Charles Bulfinch, who gets credit for the State House and just about every other very important building in town, are still occupied by some of the Old Families. And along with them, Beacon Hill is still a symbol of wealth and privilege, a place from which one can look down on the rabble and over to the State House for help in keeping the rabble in their place.

The upwardly-mobile Irish of the 20's, it should be mentioned, found their place outside Boston, in suburbs like Brookline, Dorchester and Jamaica Plain.

Among the broad avenues and high-rise buildings of Boston nestles the First Church of Christ, Scientist left.

Most of the houses on Beacon Hill were in place and occupied by people with a high idea of their place in life before Irish immigrants began arriving in huge numbers in the early 19th century. Mount Vernon Street, where the television series was filmed, is one of the best on the Hill and an absolute joy for strollers. It's a happy mix of Classical and Federal architecture with a little sprinkling of Victorian just to keep you smiling. Each building, not just on this street, but all over the Hill, has a personality of its own. But together they're like a Vivaldi concerto with the State House a virtuoso solo instrument.

Wrought iron fences and balconies soften stone and brick; gas lights make shadows dance. In summer, red geraniums and green ivy spill out of window boxes. In winter, especially at Christmas, the light and warmth comes at you through high mullioned windows. It's city life as city life was meant to be!

One of the houses on the Hill is a little lower than the rest because the lot it stands on had been owned by the man across the street who made it a condition of the sale that no structure on it could be more than 13-feet high. After all, anything higher would spoil his view. Down the block, the seller of some lots made the buyer agree to set his buildings back off the street so he wouldn't be blocked from his view of the Charles River. Who could blame either of them? But where in the world but Boston could you find buyers who would agree to such demands?

John Hancock's house on the Hill was torn down some years ago and replaced by another whose owners took their old address from down the street. The Architectural Commission would have saved it today, but when it was offered for sale to the state as a landmark, it was turned down because the price was too high.

Not far from it is the Boston Athenaeum, one of the world's great libraries. Among other things, it contains George Washington's personal book collection, each with Washington's book plate and his signature. It's a strictly private library, founded by Daniel Webster and others, including Ralph Waldo Emerson's father, open only to the gentlemen who support it and the scholars who need it.

Gentlemen and scholars! The words go with Boston as easily as clams go with beer!

It wasn't always the case. Back in 1624, not long after Pilgrims had settled themselves down in Plymouth, a ship full of indentured servants arrived in Massachusetts Bay. Their leader, Thomas Morton, freed them and invited them to settle down with him in a town he called Merriemount. They were all from Elizabethan England and had quite different ideas about life from the Puritans who preceded them. They loved a good time. They thought it was great fun to go fishing and hunting and not do much else. As a result, the Indians adored them.

They hadn't been there three years when Morton decided it was time they had a big party. After all, hadn't the Pilgrims put together a three-day feast at harvest time a few years before? May Day was the day he picked, and as a centerpiece for the party, they built an 80-foot maypole topped with deer antlers. Then the fun began. William Bradford, of Plymouth, said in his History that they were "drinking and dancing about it many days together, inviting the Indean woman for their consorts, dancing and frisking togither like so many faeries, and worse practices." Sounds like more fun than Thanksgiving? Shame on you!

It was all too much for the long-suffering Plymouth Puritans. But they were a peaceful lot, and they held their peace. Then it was discovered that the Merriemount settlers were selling guns to the Indians. The Puritans dispatched a force under the command of one Captain Miles Standish to drive them back where they came from.

They ordered Morton to surrender, but he hurled back an insult instead, calling poor little Miles Standish "Captain Shrimpe." Standish attacked and easily defeated them. They were soon loaded on a passing ship and sent back to England. Standish admitted later the defeat was easy because they were "over armed with drinke."

And so, thanks to Demon Rum, Massachusetts Bay was made safe for God-fearing people. And it wouldn't be long before they arrived.

The settlers who followed were Puritans like the people who had built the colony at Plymouth.

But not exactly the same. In Plymouth, their brand of Puritanism removed them completely from the Church of England, which they felt was far too Roman. The new breed felt the same, but believed they should remain Anglicans and work from within to change it.

They formed a company called the Massachusetts Bay Company, which was chartered to settle and to trade, with a heavy emphasis on the latter. They arrived in the summer of 1629 and settled in a place they called Salem, meaning "house of peace."

Up until that time, most of the American colonies were run by trading companies head-quartered in London. The directors of the Massachusetts Bay Company, apparently believing their own P.R., decided to move themselves to America, too. That way, they had less interference from the Crown and the Church back home. It gave them control over their own destiny.

And so, in 1630, John Winthrop, Lord of Groton Manor and head of the Massachusetts Bay Company, arrived in Salem with 400 settlers and an urge to take over. Rather than settling in Salem, which was already overcrowded, they moved down the bay and established a string of settlements, one of which they called Boston.

Within the next ten years, another 20,000 followed them!

Winthrop's brand of Puritanism attracted middle- and upper-class businessmen, who sold out their interests back home and as a result arrived with some cash in their pockets. "Send us your poor..." was not a slogan the Massachusetts Bay Company would have used. The newcomers' cash bought food and housing and then went back to England to pay for things they needed but couldn't produce for themselves. Also, because they were businessmen, it was only natural they should stick to their last in the new country. In no time at all, they were trading fish for Virginia tobacco and shipping it off to England. They were shipping fish to Portugal and coming back loaded with wine. They had established themselves as princes. And that made them the Establishment in colonial America. Gentlemen to the core. And scholars, of course. One of the first things they learned was that rum was in great demand in Africa. And that Africans were in great demand in the West Indies, which is where the sugar comes from to make rum. They got the message, and for a long time Boston produced more rum than any city in the world.

But that's not to say that scholarship in Boston was only restricted to chasing money. The Puritans believed that anyone who couldn't read was at the very least Satan's tool, and most likely doomed to damnation and hellfire. To prevent it, one of their first acts was to build a school in Boston, modelled after the ones they knew in England. They called it the Boston Latin School, and it became the model for public education all over the United States. The idea was to teach youngsters to read the Bible for themselves so they wouldn't have to get the Word by hearsay. It was only for boys, mind you. Not that they didn't want to keep their daughters from the Devil's clutches; but most girls could learn to read at their mother's knee, while they were learning needle-point and all those other essential arts. If mom was too busy, and the family rich enough, there were private schools for girls, and they taught social dancing along with reading and writing.

The Massachusetts Bay people were even more concerned about the future of their church than the future of their children, and fretted about what might happen if the supply of preachers ran out. Every town needed one, and there were plenty of good men in England who wanted the jobs. But in the long run, they knew they had better develop some home-grown product.

One of the preachers brought over from England was a man named John Harvard, who died within a year of arriving. He was so impressed by the idea of establishing a college that he left his library and half his fortune, about £400, in his will to get the ball rolling. It impressed the colonists enough to name the place after him, and the General Court enough to match his grant out of tax receipts.

The new college was established in a place called Newtown. But probably as a gesture to give it confidence and a tradition to live up to, they quickly changed the name to Cambridge.

John Harvard wouldn't recognize the place today, any more than he'd recognize himself in the wonderful, but not historically accurate, statue of him by Daniel Chester French. The old town common is partly preserved in Harvard Square, but new buildings of just about every period have taken up the space that was originally left between the houses. A great many fine colonial buildings still stand in Cambridge, but even the oldest is some 50 years younger than Harvard itself. And a great many buildings that look colonial may have been built when your grandfather was a boy. Some of the buildings are Victorian, many are Gothic. It all depends on what was in style when they were built.

The oldest building on the Harvard campus is the Georgian Massachusetts Hall, built in 1718, and its mate, Harvard Hall, built about 50 years later. They faced the Cambridge Common until the 1880's, when Stanford White built Johnson Gate and the fence that goes with it. All the great architects seem to have contributed to the Harvard Campus. Charles Bulfinch's University Hall, Ware and Van Brunt's landmark Memorial Hall, H.H. Richardson's masterpiece Sever Hall, Horace Trumbauer's Widener Library, McKim, Mead & White's Robinson Hall and William Morris Hunt's Hunt Hall are all monuments to men who gave the country style. The great 20th century builders are represented here, too. Walter Gropius led the way and Cambridge is dotted with the work of such men as Edward D. Stone, Philip Johnson, I.M. Pei, Hugh Stubbins and others.

The first major reinforced concrete structure ever built is at Harvard, but it wasn't built by a modern architect. It's the Harvard Stadium, built in 1903 on an idea of Ira Nelson Hollis, a Harvard engineering professor.

Those big white buildings you see when you cross Harvard Bridge from Boston to Cambridge aren't Harvard buildings at all, but part of another institution any city would be proud of, Massachusetts Institute of Technology. A few of its buildings reflect the Beaux Arts style that was popular when MIT moved over from Boston in 1913, but most of it has the modern look of the work of men like Eduardo Catalano, Hugh Stubbins, Pietro Belluschi and Emery Roth. It's what goes on inside those buildings that's really important. Much of the atom bomb development and other technology of the Second World War happened here, and many of the ideas that put men on the moon came from the MIT scientists. Most important for all the rest of New England is that the brainpower centered in Cambridge attracts industry to the area in the form of companies who need to have a jump on all the latest developments.

But Harvard is where tradition lives. And some of the traditions leave outsiders scratching their heads. Back in the 19th century, it was a rule there that "no scholar shall go out of his chamber without coate, gown or cloake; and it should be modest and sober habit without strange ruffian-like or newfangled fashions, without any lavish dresse or excess of apparrell whatsoever."

From that came a rule that no freshman could wear his hat in Harvard Yard "unless it rains, hails or snows, provided he be on foot and have not both hands full."

Until recently, another tradition was that Harvard was for men only. Women, you see, enrolled in Radcliffe. They were taught by Harvard professors and Harvard's president signed their diplomas, which always bore the Harvard seal. Radcliffe and Harvard finally "got married," and a Radcliffe girl is as much a Harvard man as anybody.

On the other side of town, Boston has a tradition that goes back to the 1770's but is as new as the 1970's. Its centerpiece is a meat market called Faneuil Hall (pronounce it like flannel), which was one of the places a bunch of hotheads used as a secret meeting place to plan a revolution a little more than 200 years ago. The area it's in is called Dock Square, and it's not far from the place where some of those hotheads dumped a lot of British tea into the harbor just before their revolutionary plans went into action.

It was the city's marketplace from the very earliest times. That's where the ships were, and people knew they could eliminate the middleman if they did their dealing right on the docks. Over the years, other markets joined the original to handle the overflow, and the most elaborate of them, Quincy Market, has recently been restored

in a $20 million effort that took six years. The restoration has given Boston the best waterfront area east of San Francisco. It's an exciting combination of food shops and restaurants, merchants selling plants and cookware, books and kitchen ware, wine, cheese and whatever else can be sold to a crowd of people with not much more on their mind than enjoying themselves.

The setting is a 550-foot long, narrow building with a three-storey copper rotunda in the middle. Pushcart vendors on the wide brick plazas on each side are protected by glass awnings that keep the weather out, but let the sunshine in. About the only thing that's missing, compared to other restored historic neighborhoods around the country, are the poster sellers, the candle dealers, the head shops and incense peddlers. But nobody really seems to miss them much. Like so many other things about Boston, it's a civilized place.

Civilization reaches another great height in Boston's Back Bay. Lewis Mumford said it is "the outstanding achievement in American urban planning for the 19th Century."

The Esplanade along the river gives its residents a place to get a breath of fresh air; the residential streets are separate from shopping streets, but not so separate as to hinder convenience; and there are commercial districts, too, so Back Bay people don't have to travel far to work. It's a neighborhood that includes McKim, Mead and White's magnificent Symphony Hall at one end, and the wonderful Public Gardens at the other. It includes Copley Square and Commonwealth Avenue, too. What city wouldn't be pleased to have either one?

The Boston Public Library is on Copley Square. McKim, Mead & White designed the original. Philip Johnson "improved" on their work in an addition he designed in 1972. Others have tried to improve Back Bay in recent years, too. The Prudential Life Insurance Company, for instance, built a complex of buildings in the 1960's that are probably best forgotten, except that the tower is so huge you can't escape it. Another insurance company, John Hancock, added its contribution with a 60-story tower. Its architect, who is probably better left nameless, envisioned an "invisible building" covered with a reflecting glass skin. Unfortunately, variable temperatures and high winds shattered the dream, and if Bostonians valued their lives they stayed away from the "windswept plaza" at the base. If they didn't get hit by flying glass, they got in the way of the sweepers. The windows that were blown out were replaced by plywood panels as a temporary measure, and the building was known as the plywood tower. The problems seem to have been corrected by now, but it's probably a good idea to make sure your life insurance is paid up if you plan to walk anywhere near it.

The Back Bay was really a bay when Winthrop and his company arrived. Or rather it was more like a marsh. As the city grew, some of the inlets were filled, but in the middle of the last century it was a mess. In 1857 the City Fathers built a special railroad over to Needham, and until the turn of the century trains went back and forth over it carrying dirt to fill in the bay. When the project was finished, people began to come down from Beacon Hill and across the Common to settle there. The Charles Street edge of the Common, all the way to Washington Street, had been the shoreline up until then. New streets like Commonwealth Avenue, which could have been imported from Paris, added to the lure of the latest thing. By the middle of the 19th century, anyone who wanted to be considered fashionable in Boston (and after all, what else was there to aspire to?), just *had* to be seen walking on Commonwealth Avenue on the way from church to a stroll through the Commons.

The Boston Common is the oldest public park in the country. It was also the object of one of the first shrewd business deals by Puritans in America. When they arrived, the whole Shawmut Peninsula, where they built Boston, was owned by a preacher who was operating on a King's grant, and had lived there for nearly ten years. As a man of God, he was happy to see these God-fearing people from the old country and he invited them to stay. They took over. Oh, they were generous with him. They let him keep 50 acres, plenty of land for a man who wasn't even a farmer. Within a few months, just to make things legal, they asked him to sell them his 50 acres. He did, gladly, for £30. But the deed he signed gave Winthrop and his company the whole peninsula. Sure, it was a low price. But even considering the value of the English pound today, it was a better deal than Peter Minuit gave the owners of Manhattan Island.

Everyone in the Colony was assessed to raise the money, and in return, the Governor decreed that the preacher's garden would henceforth be common property. And he was as good as his word. It still is.

At first, it was used as a pasture for the colonists' cows and a parade ground for their militia. Not much later, it was used for public executions and punishment of one sort or another. As in England at the time, a good hanging was a great crowd-pleaser, In Boston they called it going to see someone "turned off." It was also considered great fun to stroll along the Common and toss rotten eggs at some pour soul who had been sentenced to "an hour in ye stocks." Oddly, the first person to use the stocks in Boston was the unfortunate carpenter who built them. The Elders thought his price was too high for the work, so they fined him the amount of his bill and locked him up for an hour.

British troops were billeted on the Common, and left from there to try to beat Paul Revere to Lexington and Concord. Some of them, like the hanging victims, are buried under it.

Though the Boston Massacre, one of the first brushes with the British before the war, took place over on State Street, the memorial to its victims is on the Common. They say it's good luck to shake the hand of Crispus Attucks, the black man who was the first to give his life for his country in the Revolutionary War. If it's true, there are a of lucky people in Boston. The hand is the best-polished piece of bronze in the city.

They say the game of football was first played on the Boston Common. It was also the place where, in 1688, an event took place that would become a political football later. Goody Glover was hanged as a witch because she had been caught saying the rosary in Gaelic in front of a "craven image" of the Virgin. All Irishmen were Devils. Everyone in Boston believed that in 1688.

One of the things that makes Boston, and all New England for that matter, unique in America is that it existed for two centuries and more with only a single culture. All the English colonies to the south of it welcomed anybody and everybody no matter where they came from. The Dutch were the originals in New York; Germans had flocked to Philadelphia; the French and Spanish were part of the established fabric almost everywhere. But Boston was quite content to stay English. In the first 20 years of the colony, some 20,000 people migrated there, and just about all of them came from England. Not only that, but almost all of them were Puritans dedicated with all their hearts to success, to God and to hard work (not necessarily in that order!).

As their numbers grew, so did the number of towns they lived in. But Boston was always at the heart of it, and no one ever dared challenge that. Later, as they began to industralize, the great Boston entrepreneurs looked out into the countryside, and where the poets among them saw laughing bubbling brooks and sparkling waterfalls they saw free energy. They changed old towns and built new ones, and for the first time farmers didn't have to feel guilty over not having enough work to do in the wintertime. There was cloth to be woven, shoes to be made. There was work to be done.

There was so much work, in fact, they needed more people to do it all. Then, as He had done so often in their view, God provided them with an answer to the problem. In 1845, Ireland was visited by a famine that wiped out more than a million people in less than five years. Rather than starve, a million-and-a-half of them left the country. In spite of what they may have thought of old England, New England was very attractive indeed. There were jobs there. And opportunities.

Within forty years, Boston had an Irish Mayor.

But what a terrible forty years it was! It was bad enough that these newcomers were Irish. One of Boston's venerable leaders wrote: "They were the scum of creation, beaten men from beaten races, representing the worst failure in the struggle for existence.... These immigrants were inferior peoples whose prolific issue threatened the very foundations of Anglo-American civilization." That was part of the rub! These new immigrants were almost all Catholics. That was

what the Puritans came to Boston to get away from. And with their views on birth control . . . well, it's only a matter of time, isn't it?

They called them "muckers" and "micks", "blacklegs" and "greenhorns." They hired their women, whom they always called "Bridget" at best, or "Biddy" at worst, to do the dirty work in their homes for $1.50 a week. Then they kept a third to pay for the board.

By the time the Irish arrived, the North End had already lost its cachet for the fashionable Yankees, and whole neighborhoods there had simply been abandoned. Irish families moved into the big old mansions, usually one to a room, which meant they shared what sanitary facilities there were among dozens of whole families. And that, in turn, meant many of them fell victim to cholera, smallpox and worse.

But if the Puritans thought they were the only people God gave gifts to, they didn't know much about God or the Irish. One of their gifts was for survival. They believed, as an article of faith, that a man's reward was in heaven. That helped them endure hardships even the toughest Yankee would have blanched at, because the Puritans believed just as strongly in the here and now, and that hardship was as much a punishment as a test.

The Irish had a gift for politics, too, and they knew how to use it. As a counter-measure, the Puritans set up residency laws and literacy laws to keep them from voting. But it was only a matter of time before that trick wouldn't work any more. They used their influence to spread stories that the Irish were nothing but drunkards, people who preferred welfare to an honest day's work, and worst of all, people who couldn't be loyal to any state because any information entrusted to them would be transmitted straight back to the Pope in Rome.

The old line leaders were, by and large, Republican in those days after the Civil War. So the Irish were Democrats. To counter that, Bostonians formed new parties that allowed them tighter control. One of them was called "The Know-Nothings," because its members usually didn't discuss what they stood for except with insiders.

They got to be so powerful that they elected a

Governor, and gained control of both the state house and the city council in a single election. It was then people discovered how little they really did know. Though they did all they could to keep the Irish down, patience won out, and eventually the door was open for them to play the game they love so much: running for office and getting elected.

On the other side of the coin, if the established Bostonians had gone to the docks to meet the Irish with brass bands and CARE Packages, there still would have been trouble. The Irish had some experience with the "Bloody British" back home, and their new hosts were, in many cases, more British than their cousins back home in Sussex. Even though without them America might have stayed a part of the British Empire to this day, they were English and proud of it. Then there was that problem of religion. To the Irish, being Protestant was much worse than being a heathen. And, of course, the Puritans were Protestant to a fault. It wasn't the first time and, unfortunately, not the last, that men used the love of God to justify hate.

By the time the Irish had gotten political clout, Boston had become different again. While all the scrapping was going on, Italians began arriving, then Lithuanians and Poles. Germans came, too, along with Portuguese, Scandinavians and French Canadians. But the Irish controlled the wards, and if you wanted a streetlight or a city job you had to go to them. And after all those years of feeling the stings of prejudice, guess who was dealing them out. Human nature is a mysterious thing.

But no matter what else Boston immigrants found, most eventually got what they came for. Freedom. It's an important part of Boston tradition.

Of all the cities in the United States, Boston is in the upper ranks among places that are good for walking. For strollers, walkers, runners, joggers, even roller skaters, Boston is their kind of town. And one of the best walks in Boston is the one they call The Freedom Trail.

It begins at the Park Street side of the Common with a monument not to the Revolutionary War, but to the Civil War, the Park Street Church. Henry James called it "the most interesting mass of brick and mortar in America". The call for the abolition of slavery went out from Boston first, and some of the most impassioned speeches were made from the pulpit here. Whether it was guilt over having made so much money in the slave trade or Puritan religious fervor, slavery was an issue all Boston responded to, and they were leaders both in the movement and in the war. Around the corner is the Old Granary Burying Ground. It's one of five in the center of the city, and a favorite place for people who get their kicks making rubbings from old headstones. You need a permit to do it, but it's worth the effort because among some of the names the rubbers pick up are John Hancock, Samuel Adams and Mother Goose. Andrew Faneuil, of Faneuil Hall fame, is resting in peace under a stone inscribed with his nephew's first initial and his own name misspelled as "Funel." Benjamin Franklin's parents are buried there, too. So is Boston's very first mayor.

Why, you might ask, is a cemetery called a "granary." It was named for a huge shed that once stood next to it, built as a store-house for surplus wheat and corn that could be distributed to the needy poor. But in the early days Boston had very few poor families and after the custodian reported that "weevils have taken the wheet, and mice annoy the corn much, being very numerous," the building was torn down and the salvage used to build a tavern. But the name lives on, so to speak, in the cemetery.

The trail goes past the Athenaeum and into School Street, where colonial youngsters got a taste of the 3R's and an occasional hickory stick at the Boston Latin School. At this point, strollers usually get a chance to sit down because the trail leads inside King's Chapel, the first Episcopal church in New England, but a Unitarian Church since Revolutionary times, also the first of that denomination. Much of the furnishings consist of gifts from English Royalty, and the interior can be called "Georgian" with no argument from anybody. In fact, it's probably the best example of Georgian decoration anywhere in New England.

The church was originally a wooden building, but was covered in local granite after the locals discovered it was a good building material. Once the stonework was finished, the old building was torn down from inside.

Not far away is the Old Corner Book Store, restored for us by yet another important Boston institution, the Boston Globe. Emerson knew the place well, so did Hawthorne and Longfellow. The old City Hall is there, too, wonderfully restored as a restaurant and office building. And not far from it, another great job of restoration, Old South Meetinghouse, now a bookstore and museum.

The Freedom Trail wanders past Faneuil Hall and the Quincy Market as well as the new City Hall, a massive pile of concrete and glazed brick. Then, mercifully, it takes you out of the way of an elevated expressway, a construction Boston seems to have in far too much abundance. And from there, it wanders back into the past for a look at the only wooden building left from the 17th century, Paul Revere's house. When it was built, it was conveniently located next to the town pump, across from the public market, near the meeting house, hard by the the local guardhouse. A lively spot indeed. Paul Revere added some contributions to the general din: he had 16 children. He did a lot of other things, too, of course. And his accomplishments are spread out for anyone who visits the house to see for themselves. The style of the house is Elizabethan English, and looks just like the homes the Puritans left behind in the old country. It also, of course, looks just like the houses they built when they got to Boston.

Most of the old houses were destroyed in a series of fires over the early years. Fire was surely their worst enemy, and it's the reason why very few authentic colonial buildings are left in any of the cities that were part of the original colonies. Urban "improvement" is another reason, too, of course. There isn't a single Dutch building left in New York, for instance. Most were destroyed by fire, but the last remaining one had an encounter with a wrecker's ball some years ago.

Just around the corner from Paul Revere's house, and an appropriate end to the Freedom Trail, is Old North Church, where Paul Revere did his famous sound and light show. It's one of the oldest churches in Boston, with bells cast in England, and for years was the highest structure

in the city, purposely made that way as a landmark for sailors. It looks a lot like the church of St. James in Piccadilly, London, and tourists in either direction usually notice the resemblance. Londoners with longer memories recognize it as a church that was once on Queen Victoria Street in London, called St. Andrews-by-the-Wardrobe with St. Anne, Blackfriars. Unfortunately, it was destroyed in the unpleasantness called the London Blitz. Some of the parishoners of North Church had come from Blackfriars, so the resemblance was more than a coincidence.

When it was built, it broke sharply with a tradition of long standing in New England. The Puritans had built meeting houses that were purposely simple, undecorative, uncomfortable. This church had a raised pulpit, galleries, divided pews and simple, but quite lovely, decoration. Popery? Some would have said so in 1723 when it was built. But by then the Puritans were ready for a little style in their religion.

We call it "Old" North Church today because of Longfellow's poem about Paul Revere's ride. Actually, it's the newer of two structures people call "North Church." The other one was chopped up for firewood by British troops billeted near there. And this one's official name is really Christ Church.

But it is old, and its style has been repeated in churches all over New England and up and down the East Coast. The steeple wasn't added until the church was more than 15 years old, but in plenty of time to be useful to Paul Revere. Like every other steeple in New England, it was built like a telescope from inside the church. As each stage got smaller, workmen's space got tighter. The spire, in this case a weather vane in the shape of a flower and pot with a banner, a ball and five-pointed star, was built on the ground and then pushed up through the hole in the top. Life was much safer, if more confining, for steeplejacks in those days.

A hurricane blew the steeple down in 1804 and it was replaced, with one some 15 feet shorter than the original, by Charles Bulfinch. The same thing happened again in 1955, and it was replaced again. This time, they had to send all the way to New Hampshire for a crane high enough to replace the weathervane. So much for progress!

During the Revolution, the North End was a hotbed of Tories, and a great many of the residents left town and headed for Canada when they saw how things were turning out. Slightly deserted, the neighborhood got less fashionable, and anyway, people were beginning to long for the open spaces of the suburbs. They moved to Beacon Hill.

By the beginning of the 19th century, the North End had been converted from Boston's most prestigious neighborhood to a district of factories making everything from cannon balls to flower pots. The workers in the factories, because there was no subway then, moved into the neighborhood, and they were followed by new arrivals from abroad.

Within a generation, the neighborhood would be called "Little Italy," and it's one of the most tightly-packed city neighborhoods anywhere in the United States. It's a section of narrow streets and alleys, tenement buildings with tomatoes and basil growing in pots on the fire escapes. Laundry flies from lines stretched between the buildings like the banners of some medieval festival. Old people with lined faces you can't resist sit outside their buildings discussing the past and the present, with their hands punctuating every sentence.

If you can make it past Quincy Market with your appetite intact, your reward is here. Stop in a groceria to take home a little home-made pasta as a souvenir of the trip. Go to a clam house for some scungilli, then next door to a Tratoria for liguini, then on to a Ristorante for the best veal cutlet limone this side of Naples. And for the crowning touch, sit in front of an outdoor café under a bright red and green umbrella and sip hot and strong espresso while you watch this wonderful world pass by and treat yourself to a sinfully sweet cannoli.

Late in the summer and well into the fall, when most visitors to New England are heading for the hills to look for fall colors, the North East gets more colorful itself. It's festa time, and the streets are decorated with colored lights. The sidewalks are covered with stands selling pizza and ravioli, zeppole and Italian cheesecake. You can try your luck at games of chance or games of skill. And if you don't enjoy yourself, it's your problem.

The whole thing comes to a peak on October 12, when Boston Italians come out in force to remind other Bostonians that an Italian, Christopher Columbus, made it here in 1492, a long, long time before those Pilgrims set foot on Plymouth Rock in 1620.

After World War II, a great many younger Italian families moved away from the North End and out into the suburbs. But the neighborhood itself has a strong lure, and some are starting to come back now that areas around it are being renewed. And that's the best kind of urban renewal there is.

Italian Opera came to Boston some years after the Italians themselves. It started seriously with a performance of *La Gioconda* as the curtain-raiser for the 1907 season. It was such a hit, the cultural establishment dispatched an architect to study all the great opera houses of Europe and to design a better one. Whether he succeeded or not is a matter for historians to debate. His opera house was torn down in 1958. But while it lasted, it represented culture par excellence to Bostonians, who turned up each season dressed in the finest clothes and most expensive jewels their money could buy.

It should be mentioned, though, that opera may still be alive and well in Boston in the hands of Sarah Caldwell and her new Boston Opera.

The Puritans didn't have a passion for music, though some of them were known to be very good dancers. Their idea of a moving musical experience was an evening of psalm singing, and their idea of entertainment was listening to a good lecture. But in the mid-19th century, their mood changed as they discovered Mozart and lyric poetry, Haydn and great books. Forty years later, Henry Lee Higginson founded the Boston Symphony Orchestra. He directed it and supported it with his own money from its founding in 1881 until 1918.

In Boston, they call it simply "symphony." Boston women who want to be somebody meet their peers every Friday all winter long at the afternoon concerts in Symphony Hall. It's a ritual Lucius Beebe said takes on "the aspect of holy days dedicated to the classics and a vast craning of necks to be certain that the Hallowells and the Forbeses are in their accustomed stalls."

In summer, "symphony" is at Tanglewood in the Berkshires, a tradition started by one of the orchestra's great conductors, Serge Koussevitzky, in 1936. The place he picked, which now also includes a summer music school, was the former summer home of Nathaniel Hawthorne.

For city-bound Bostonians, the Hatch Memorial Bandshell on the Charles River is where to find the sounds of summer. All during the month of July, the Boston Pops entertains in free concerts there. It's a tradition, like the orchestra itself, begun by the late Arthur Fiedler, himself one of Boston's real treasures. The Pops Concerts are held inside Symphony Hall in the spring. But the real highlight of the year, for the Pops and for all of Boston is their Fourth of July concert on the river, complete with fireworks and their trademark, *The Stars and Stripes Forever.*

In summer, the grassy esplanade along the Charles River is a haven for joggers, sunbathers and lovers. At night, they stroll along Copley Plaza to listen to street musicians or sit on the steps of the Public Library to discuss among themselves what a wonderful place this city is. Or maybe they go down to the waterfront to pick up a breeze and a little wine and cheese.

Office workers spend their lunch hours on the plaza outside City Hall, grabbing a snack from a sidewalk vendor and relaxing to the sounds of a bluegrass fiddle or an electric piano or both competing with each other.

It's always had the reputation of a livable city, but Boston may not have been more livable at any time in her history than right now. People who move there from other cities stay there. People who discover it as students keep going back to recharge their mental batteries. Quite simply, people who like cities love Boston.

It has its detractors, of course. What city doesn't? But people who find fault usually don't understand cities and don't care to. One of the most common comments you hear from them is that they aren't safe. Well, when someone asked the mayor of Boston if he wasn't worried about the possibility that places like Quincy Market might be a haven for purse-snatchers, he gave the answer the question deserved:

"If you're worried about handbag snatchers," he said, "you can live in the Berkshires."

And you'll never know what you're missing.

Sheathed in mirrors to reduce its apparent size, the Hancock Tower right rises 60 stories high above the tranquil Charles River.

Boston is a city in which the historical and the modern stand side by side. On these pages and overleaf the broad avenues and expressways of today's metropolis merge with the narrow streets which separate the houses of old Boston, and the modernity of Logan International Airport and of a skyline studded with skyscrapers contrasts with historic churches and the gracious vestiges of colonial days.

Boston Harbor above, *at the mouths of the Charles and Mystic Rivers, is an important port with forty miles of piers, docks and wharves. Yet the Charles River these pages and overleaf is still one of the most picturesque sights of Boston. It is also a popular haunt for boating enthusiasts and, as the day draws on, the sails of countless yachts are silhouetted against the evening sky.*

Modern hotels and office blocks and streamlined highways and bridges *these pages and overleaf* are now very much part of Boston, but the old brick mansions of colonial days still stand, mellow red along tree-lined streets, and Boston Common *above right* remains as the oldest public park in the country.

27

Boston's shopping facilities are justly renowned and the Charles Street neighborhood, at the foot of Beacon Hill, is particularly noted for its antique stores, arts and crafts shops, specialty boutiques and restaurants shown *left, above and right.* Established in 1826, the Union Restaurant below and *above right, is the oldest restaurant in the city.*

Beacon Hill, one of the country's oldest residential neighborhoods on these pages, has retained its narrow, cobblestone streets and its red-brick houses in a charming historic area, now designated a National Landmark.

The focal point of the Hill is the Massachusetts State House with its magnificent golden dome overleaf. The central brick portion was designed by Charles Bulfinch and the cornerstone was laid in 1795 by Governor Samuel Adams assisted by Paul Revere.

Most of the building on Beacon Hill occurred in the early 18th century when three hills of the area were leveled to create a neighborhood which has to this day retained its charmingly traditional atmosphere.

Copp's Hill Burying Ground above and above left is Boston's second oldest cemetery. Three signers of the Declaration of Independence are buried in Granary Burying Ground far right, among them Paul Revere whose statue is shown right in North End. Beyond the trees of Boston Common left and overleaf rises the spire of Park Street Church while on the site of the first Town House below stands the Old State House.

Outside the State House a flag flies above among luxurious gardens. Opposite the house a monument left pays tribute to Robert Gauld Shaw and the black 54th Regiment.

Boston Common, site of the Soldiers and Sailors Monument below is also the scene of the Annual Loyalty Day Program, in which the Ladies' Auxiliary to the Veterans of the Foreign Wars of the U.S. right dedicate their allegiance to the democratic traditions of liberty and justice.

Winter ices the Charles River and brings snow to the Boston streets overleaf.

The Charles River and Boston Harbor on these pages *with the Community Boathouse* above right *provide an idyllic setting for countless pleasure craft of all kinds.*

Viewed from across the Charles River overleaf, *the Prudential Tower soars 750 feet above the boathouse.*

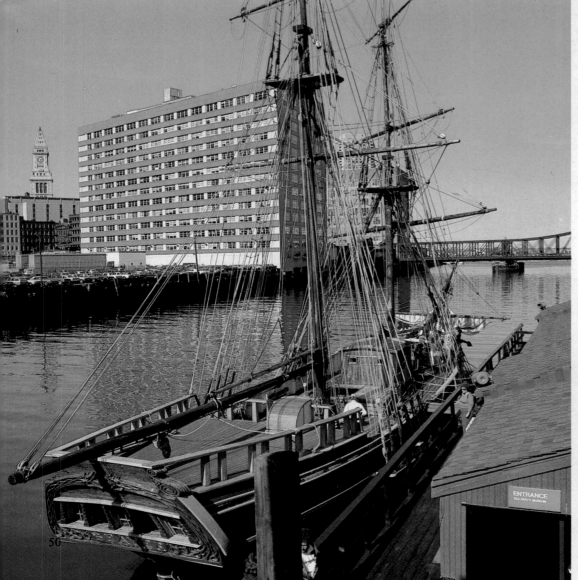

Boston's historical background, so closely associated with the sea, is perhaps most keenly felt along the waterfront area. Here the Brig Beaver II above and left, an authentic replica of one of three ships involved in the notorious Boston Tea Party, is open to members of the public who can relive history by tossing tea-chests overboard, in imitation of the Colonial rebels.

The U.S. Frigate Constitution below and right, known as "Old Ironsides" because the cannon balls bounced off her sides, was rebuilt and restored in 1833 and is now moored at Boston Naval Shipyard.

51

The Boston Tea Party Ship recalls that historic day when a group of men dressed as "Indians" gathered at Griffin's Wharf and methodically broke open chests of tea, spilling their contents into the harbor.

53

Founded by Mary Baker Eddy in 1879 to "reinstate primitive Christianity and its element of healing", the First Church of Christ, Scientist on these pages and overleaf is the world headquarters of the Christian Science Church. It is set in the middle of an impressive new center, designed by architects Pei and Cossutta.

Boston's Back Bay, which until 1860 was nothing but tidal mud flats on the Charles River, is now one of the most impressive areas of the city. In addition to imposing stone and brick mansions the district includes among other enterprising products of modern design the Christian Science Church Complex above left and right and a backbone of new skyscrapers above. In the midst of these, the 52 story Prudential Tower, tallest in New England, rises from a reflecting pool spanned by four bridges.

Equally striking in their modernity are the Government Center Plaza below and the New Boston City Hall left. Designed by architects Kallman, McKinnell and Knowles, the hall was opened in 1969 amid a storm of controversy and dubbed an "Aztec Tomb" by its critics.

More traditional in style, the Massachusetts State House overleaf still enshrines the battle flags carried by Massachusetts' troops.

The tranquility of the riverbank above left contrasts with the bustle of North Station center left, with downtown bottom and with the city's concrete congestion above and below right, while among the high rise buildings the spire of Park Street Church above serves as a reminder of a bygone era.

The Old Corner Bookstore left has housed book-sellers or publishers since 1712 and Faneuil Hall Marketplace above dates from 1846 when Mayor Quincy first opened a city-owned marketplace.

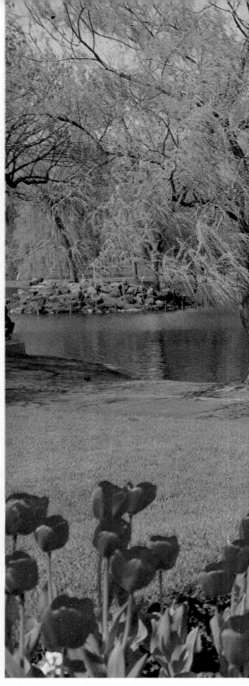

In the very heart of the city the Public Garden provides an oasis of fountains, formal flower beds and rare trees. It is particularly famous for its Swanboats above, right and center left and for its monuments to great men of the Republic, such as the equestrian statue of George Washington below and below left.

Reflected below in the mirror-like walls of the soaring John Hancock Tower right, Trinity Church above stands in historic Copley Square. Designed by Henry Hobson Richardson, it is a free adaptation of 11th-century French Romanesque style and its magnificent interior left is marked by a series of exquisite stained-glass windows.

Boston's skyscrapers rise in silhouette against the evening sky as sunset tints the snow-covered city overleaf.

Some of Boston's finest architecture is to be found in its many lovely churches, among them Trinity Church below, the Christian Science Church center left and the Old South Church top left. The Old South Meeting House top, now part of the Boston Historical Park, once housed the congregation of the Third Church of Boston, and King's Chapel above is the oldest Anglican Church in New England.

Inside the magnificent State House, designed by Charles Bulfinch in 1795, are the Senate Chamber right, the marble-floored Memorial Hall below left and the House of Representatives above right, where above the carved mahogany walls paintings detail events in the history of Massachusetts.

Urban freeways, overlooked by the John Hancock Tower overleaf, pay tribute to the design of a more recent era.

Boston is a city of great variety and color and Chinatown in particular above and top, *with its distinctive pagoda-shaped telephone booths, is a place of unique charm and atmosphere.*

Haymarket, Boston's open air fruit and vegetable market *left, above, right and below has been operating for 200 years in Dock Square. On Fridays and Saturdays from dawn to dusk crowds jostle among the stalls for a variety of goods sold at wholesale prices.*

The lower floors of Faneuil Hall *below left also provide an historic marketplace. The second floor is a meeting hall of which Hack once aptly wrote: "Here Orators in ages past have mounted their attack Undaunted by proximity of sausage on the rack."*

Quincy Market on these pages *was the product of the first of many harbor landfills. In the early 1820s Mayor Josiah Quincy filled part of the cove between Long Wharf and the Town Dock and on the new land Alexander Parris designed a majestic granite market building flanked by warehouses, which today have all the atmosphere of a bazaar.*

By night Boston's skyline overleaf *presents an array of glittering lights.*

The Paul Revere House right in North Square was purchased by the master silversmith in 1770 and is the oldest wooden structure in Boston. Its delightful interior above, below right and bottom contains many of the original furnishings.

In a tiny park in James Rego Square a statue below commemorates Paul Revere's famous ride on the night of April 18th, 1775, when he warned the city's residents of the invading Redcoats.

Boston Public Library left, completed in 1895, is one of the largest and finest libraries in the country.

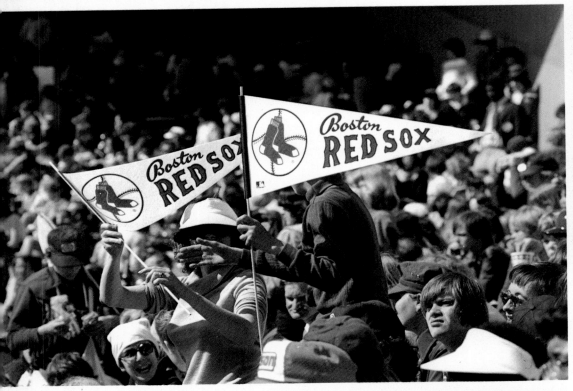

Boston is a Mecca for spectator sports enthusiasts and with four major league teams, three of which are championship winners, Bostonians are justly proud of their sporting achievements. The Red Sox baseball team, who have twice won the coveted pennant, are featured on these pages on their home ground at Fenway Park, a magnificent stadium shown from the air overleaf.

Opened in 1980, the John F. Kennedy Library on these pages *pays an impressive tribute to the Kennedy administration.*

The Museum of Science overleaf *displays exhibits on natural history, physical science, medicine and astronomy.*

From September through May, Boston's colleges and universities supplement the city's professional sporting activities, and included among the best known university teams are the Harvard University football players, seen on these pages in a match at Harvard Stadium.

Founded in 1636, Harvard University on these pages is America's oldest institution of higher learning. It is named after John Harvard, a Puritan minister who bequeathed half his estate and his library to the university and a statue on the campus below commemorates this act of generosity. Harvard Yard above was the original center of the college.

First published 1980 by Colour Library International Ltd.
© 1980 Illustrations and text: Colour Library International Ltd., 163 East 64th St., New York, N.Y.10021.
Colour separations by FERCROM, Barcelona, Spain.
Display and text filmsetting by Focus Photoset, London, England.
Printed and bound by JISA-RIEUSSET, Barcelona, Spain.
ISBN 0-8317-0980-4 Library of Congress Catalogue Card No. 79-90595
Published in the United States of America by Mayflower Books, Inc., New York City.

D.L.B.11959